The Book of the Shepherd

harperstudio

An Imprint of HarperCollins*Publishers*

The Book of the Shepherd

THE STORY OF ONE SIMPLE PRAYER, AND HOW IT CHANGED THE WORLD

By the Scribe

As discovered by JOANN DAVIS

With illustrations by SUDI MCCOLLUM

HarperCollins books may be purchased for educational, business, or sales promotional use. For information please write: Special Markets Department, HarperCollins Publishers, 10 East 53rd Street, New York, NY 10022.

For more information about this book or other books from HarperStudio, go to www.theharperstudio.com.

FIRST EDITION

Designed by Eric Butler
Illustrations by Sudi McCollum

Library of Congress Cataloging-in-Publication Data

Davis, Joann, 1953–
    The book of the Shepherd : the story of one simple prayer and how it changed the world / Joann Davis.—1st ed.
        p. cm.
    ISBN 978-0-06-173230-0
    1. Boys—Fiction. 2. Shepherd—Fiction. 3. Women slaves—Fiction. 4. Voyages and travels—Religious aspects. 5. Parables. I. Title.
PS3604.A9635B66 2009
813'.6—dc22

2009030669

09 10 11 12 13   OV/RRD   10 9 8 7 6 5 4 3 2 1

For the recklessly generous
and the relentlessly kind

For Kenny, Jenny, and Colin

Contents

Contents

Editor's Note to the Reader

HE CIRCUMSTANCES SURROUNDING *The Book of the Shepherd* are rare—even mysterious.

They began in 2007, when I bought an old farmhouse in Dorset, Vermont, from the estate of Professor Orlando Roberts, a distinguished teacher of classics at nearby Bennington College. The professor, a bachelor, had lived alone in the house for nearly fifty years. Upon signing the purchase agreement, I learned that he had no heirs and had stipulated that the contents of his house become the property of whomever bought it.

To be honest, I had no idea what I was getting myself into. In the euphemistic language of real estate, the place was a fixer-upper. In truth, it was a wreck. Full of leaky faucets and creaky doors, the house was also a cache of files, trunks, books, and portfolios scattered about in nearly every room. Weeding out the old professor's study alone looked like a job that was going to take several days.

It was in the study that I found it. Bound in vellum, the book had an image of a shepherd pressed into it. I later learned that the text was written in an unusual hybrid of Middle English and Dutch. Tucked inside the pages was a piece of Professor Roberts's personal stationery bearing the words, "Purchased in Old Barn Bookshop, Route 7. Must get translated."

The note was dated December 25, 2007, a poignant Christmas for all in the historic village of Dorset, it turned out, because it was the day that their long-time neighbor "Old Orly" died at his desk, poetically slumped over a stack of holiday greeting cards, in front of the fireplace. Old Orly's heart, known for its warmth and generosity, had simply given out.

Needless to say, I was stunned, mystified—and possessed of an obligation to do as Professor Roberts had intended. Securing translation experts from some of the greatest universities, I spent a year readying this work for publication.

Was it worth my time? Each reader must decide.

—JOANN DAVIS

Dorset, Vermont, 2008

The Book of the Shepherd

The Law Must Be Obeyed

E WAS A SMALL BOY, AS TENDER-
hearted and as innocent as a spring
lamb. He was a good boy, who said
his prayers and respected his
elders. But on this day, he was a frightened boy who
was about to feel the white hot sting of a switch
across the back of his legs.

"Please, Father," the boy cried out, "have mercy
on me."

But the man was angry. He had asked the boy
to rise at dawn to stock the market stall with fresh
fruits and vegetables. The boy was eager to honor his

father's wishes but had overslept. Now the market was teeming with customers and there was no food.

"No olives or figs?" asked a perplexed woman with a basket on her back. "No raisins or honey? What trick is this?"

The merchant tried to appease the woman, telling her to return later in the day for the sweetest delights at the lowest prices. But when she emptied her coin purse at a competitor's stall, the merchant exploded.

"You lazy boy," he said, grabbing his son by the throat and throttling him. "You take bread from my mouth. Now I must teach you a lesson you will never forget."

As the hot sun beat down, the marketplace was springing to life. Weavers were bartering with their customers. Potters were spinning at their wheels. And friends walked arm in arm through the market aisles, laughing and chatting.

But there was no joy for the merchant—only blind rage—as he took a switch usually reserved for a reluctant donkey from the back of his wagon.

"You stupid boy," he cried as he prepared to strike. "My laws must be obeyed."

Like a storm at sea gathering strength, the man's anger became uncontrollable. Lashing out, he knocked the boy to the ground, bruising and battering him. The child rolled away, trying to evade the stick, but it kept biting his flesh in a relentless flurry of blows.

The scuffle jolted the still-sleepy market like a rude rooster. A lethargic public was soon aroused and many began streaming to the food stall where the beating was happening. Some were chanting, "Beat the boy! Make him pay."

Only one in the crowd seemed to have the child in mind.

A shepherd who had been at the market well

watering his sheep had dropped everything and rushed to the scene when he heard what sounded like a crying child. He had left his animals alone at the trough to go and help.

But along the way, the shepherd became trapped in the throng, slowed by rowdy hecklers, jeering spectators, and curiosity seekers. As he tried to elbow his way forward through the thick press of sweaty bodies, he heard an old man quoting the law for filial infractions, saying "woe betide the child who disobeys his father."

When the shepherd finally broke through, he saw what he did not wish to imagine. The boy was in the dirt beneath the merchant. Still animated, still chasing him, the merchant continued to strike as the boisterous crowd made known its bloodthirsty wishes.

"Beat him!" someone shouted. "Beat him!"

The boy was grimacing—trying to squirm away—but there was no escaping the cruel switch. Whipping through the air, scourging him, the stick nipped the boy's tender skin the way the thorny bramble often gashed the flesh of lambs gamboling in the wilderness.

The shepherd's first impulse was to stop the madness, to lunge forward to protect this boy. He wanted to grab the switch from the merchant's hand and bring the cruelty to an abrupt halt. But he hesitated, questioning himself, asking what standing he had in this matter. Did the law not permit harsh measures? What would the elders say?

The thoughts were flashing through his head like intense lightning bolts across a torrid summer sky.

And then, shaking him from his stupor, he heard the boy cry out, "Mercy, Father," a wail that pierced both the air and the shepherd's heart. And then he knew.

No one had the right to cause this boy to suffer so.

No law permitted this pain to be inflicted.

Taking hold of himself, the shepherd broke through the crowd to go to the boy's aid.

But it was too late. Without warning, the merchant had put down his switch. Pure and simple, he had grown tired of beating the boy. Hot and spent, he simply laid down the stick and went to get himself a drink of water.

The crowd, disappointed that the action was over, slowly dispersed. Rushing forward, the shepherd went to assist the boy, who was still on the ground. Biting his lip, fighting back tears, the boy tried to be strong as his father had taught him to be. Gamely collecting himself, he rose to his feet and accepted a sip of water from the shepherd's pouch before letting the kind man tend to his cuts and welts. Little was said by either, but much was shared by both before the boy went on his way.

That night, when the merchant broke bread, his brother asked him about his day. "Very ordinary," the man said. "No different from any other."

A Still, Small Voice

 *TONE THE BUILDER WHO ERECTS A house that falls on its occupants.*

Sever the hands of the criminal who pilfers livestock or grain or another's garment.

Whip the child who defies an elder. For such is the law and the law must be obeyed.

For generations, these ironclad rules had governed the people. Nobody questioned whether it was right to humiliate a child or execute a murderer. An eye for an eye was the way of the world.

But was there another way?

The shepherd wondered. As he lay outstretched in an open field, beneath a blanket of twinkling stars, he reviewed the day. It had begun in a nearby town where a farmer was stoned for selling a sick cow. Each time a rock struck the man, a bloodthirsty crowd sent up a loud, enthusiastic cheer.

Later in the morning, the shepherd was in a village where two families were feuding over a cracked water jug. The potter who had sold the broken jar claimed he had made an honest mistake. But he was marched to a whipping post and given forty lashes as spectators hissed and spat at him.

Then the shepherd had assisted a young boy after a merciless beating by his father. It was all done in strict accordance with the law. But it was enough to make any God-fearing person wonder where God had been this day. Why hadn't God sent help to spare the child?

The shepherd closed his eyes and was drifting off to sleep when he thought he heard a still, small voice whispering in his ear, "I did send help. I sent you."

As Light as a Feather

HE SHEPHERD SLEPT.

He dreamed he was in a far-off place of green pastures. There were no thorny bushes in this place to prick his sheep, or ditches in which to fall. Most peculiar of all, a wizened Old Man was sitting on a wooden chest at a fork in the road, giving directions.

"Hello," said the Old Man. "Are you searching for something?"

"How did you know?" the shepherd asked.

"By that look on your face. Many of the people who come here are looking to discover the new way.

I can direct you to it. But first you'll need to have your heart weighed."

The shepherd watched as the Old Man took out a balancing scale from the trunk.

"Now," the Old Man said, scratching his head, "where's that feather?"

The Old Man was as happy as a child in a toy maker's shop as he set the feather on one side of the balancing scale. Then he reached inside the shepherd's chest and took out his heart, which was pulsing at a nice, healthy clip.

"What are you doing?" the shepherd asked.

"Don't worry," the Old Man said. "It's attached to you by an invisible gold thread so nothing bad can happen." The Old Man then paused and stepped back. "Right, then. Now, let's weigh them up," he said, setting the heart on the scale opposite the feather.

The shepherd looked on in wonder. Seeing his

own beating heart was quite mysterious, but also very natural.

Instantly, the side of the scale on which the heart was resting dipped down a little.

"Hmmm," said the Old Man. "A little heavy. Have you been discouraged?"

"Does it matter?" the shepherd asked.

"Very much," the Old Man said. "It's better to travel light, without sadness, anger, or fear. Without jealousy, judgment, or spite."

"What must I do?" the shepherd asked.

"Each morning, when you awaken, promise the dawn that you'll keep your heart as light as a feather. Commit again each night at sunset."

"And if I do?" the shepherd asked.

But the Old Man had vanished. The dream was done.

Map to the Treasure

HE NEXT MORNING, UPON SEEING the sun come up, the shepherd promised the dawn that he would keep his heart as light as a feather. Then he put on his sandals, grazed and watered his sheep, and set off on the high road that wended its way out of the village. His goal was to find the boy and to make sure that the storm clouds had passed.

"How are you?" the shepherd called out when he saw the youngster standing with his donkey in front of a small dwelling made of baked white bricks. The boy was no bigger than a sack of wheat. He had black hair and blue eyes and one of his legs was wrapped in a white bandage.

"He is fine" came a sweet, high-pitched voice.

It belonged to a woman who was young and olive-skinned, probably in her early twenties. She emerged from the dwelling, wondering if this unexpected visitor was the man who had helped the boy in the market the prior day. He was tall, lean, and well muscled, with a staff in one hand, a side bag over his shoulder, and a flock of sheep gathered around his feet.

Wary of strangers, the young woman at first kept her distance, standing back until she saw the shepherd begin to run his fingers through each of his animals' coats, gently combing for burrs and bristles.

"How well you care for your animals," she said, watching his tender hand caress the sheep.

"And they for me," the shepherd replied. "They keep me company when I am lonely. And they warm me at night when I am cold."

He introduced himself as Joshua, son of Isaac, and said he was on a journey. Then he reached out to the boy, David, and ruffled his hair affectionately, as he would a lamb. The boy drew close to him.

"Where are you going?" the woman asked, giving her name as Elizabeth. Her blue eyes sparkled and she brushed back her raven hair, revealing the fine features of a small, round face.

"I'm not certain. But I feel that I must seek a new way," the shepherd said. "I have dreamed of it."

"My grandfather spoke of the new way as he lay dying," the woman offered. "Grandfather predicted that an age of miracles would come when it is re-discovered."

The shepherd's eyes widened in astonishment.

They were dark brown like the shoulder-length hair that framed his friendly open face.

"Grandfather wanted to make the journey to find it himself," the woman continued, "but he was blind and sick by the time he came into possession of the map."

"This map," said the shepherd, "where is it now?"

"With me," the woman said. "I keep it hidden in my well."

"Why such care?" the shepherd asked.

"The new way is powerful," the woman said. "And the powerful fear it. It can change everything."

The woman's words filled the shepherd with a greater sense of urgency and purpose than he had ever before experienced. Who was this woman? She had a special glow about her and she made him feel at home. *At ease.* He felt little seeds of friendship being planted as they spoke.

But before he had a chance to say any more, the

woman led him to a small table set in the open air by the side of the house. The sun was high and hot but the table was in the shade of an old olive tree that was in full bloom. The birds were darting in and out of the branches, building a nest of twigs and leaves. The woman showed him that she had prepared a spread of figs, dates, cheese, and milk and invited him to join them.

Joshua accepted, but looked at the house. It seemed dark and empty. Perhaps David's father was off in the field and would soon be returning home.

"The merchant," Joshua asked, when the boy was out of earshot. "Do you expect him?"

"No time soon," Elizabeth said. "Still angry at what happened in the market, David's father has disowned him. I am his keeper now." Then she explained that she and the boy had been told to find a new dwelling.

Overwhelmed by sadness, the shepherd shook his head. He wondered how the merchant's heart had become a lockbox of hostility. How had it become so misshapen?

Elizabeth noticed the sorrow in Joshua's eyes. After the meal was eaten, she sent David to fetch his flute and her tambourine from the house. Then she tapped out a lively rhythm and they all danced and laughed until their bellies ached.

When the afternoon sun had moved to the western sky, Joshua asked for permission to sleep in the hayloft. His plan was to set out early the next day.

Elizabeth agreed readily and then surprised him.

"May we join you on your journey?" she asked.

Beginning the Journey

ND SO IT HAPPENED THAT THEY began their walk, guided by the map retrieved from a clay pot hidden at the bottom of the well.

They passed through villages and towns. They trekked up hills and mountains. And by the end of the first day, they found themselves in a distant hamlet. It was there that they met the Storyteller.

He was seated on the ground beneath a billowing canopy in the public square. Short in stature but stately in bearing, he wore a gold sash around the waist of his lily-white tunic and a bright red turban piled high on top of his head. Around him were stacks of leather-bound books, reams of papyrus, quill pens, and inks of many colors.

"Sit down! Join in!" the Storyteller called out, gesturing to some pillows scattered around him. As if he had been expecting guests, he had laid out bread, fish, wine, and olive oil, enough to feed a small gathering. "My table is rich and I welcome your company," he said.

"Thank you for your generosity, friend," the shepherd said. "Our stomachs are empty but so are our purses. How can we repay you?" As he spoke, his stomach rumbled. David and Elizabeth both looked expectant.

"A story would suffice," the man said. "I make my living telling them. And I never tire of hearing them."

So they ate and drank their fill. And then the shepherd told a tale.

❧ *The Shepherd's Tale*

"THERE ONCE WAS a boy who felt most at home in the barn in the springtime when a sheep or a pig or a cow was giving birth. Usually these births were routine, if bloody, affairs—long hours of hard labor followed by a happy boy clutching a newborn against his chest.

"But once, after a litter of lambs had been born, the boy's father sounded grave and called for water.

" 'Are you going to cleanse the eyes?' the boy asked innocently.

" 'No,' his father answered. 'A runt has been born.'

" 'Why do you need water?' the boy asked.

" 'To put it out of its misery,' the man said.

" 'You mean you are going to drown it?' the boy asked. He became distraught and begged his father to drown him instead.

" 'Don't be foolish,' the father scoffed. 'To survive

in the world you will need to develop a thicker hide, like that of the cattle.'

"Now this boy was a persistent boy who did not take no for an answer. He continued to plead to be allowed to keep the runt, which was so small it practically fit into the palm of his hand.

"'Silly child,' the father said. But he was tired of arguing and relented.

"In the days that followed, the boy fashioned a nest of old cloth and fed the runt two times a day with milk from the runt's mother. In the beginning, the runt did not open its eyes but always sniffed the air when the boy approached. The local herdsmen guffawed when they heard that the boy let the runt suck milk from his fingers. 'What fool lets his son become a nursemaid to a blind and dumb runt?' they asked.

"Over time, the runt became as strong and as

healthy as its siblings. One day, after nearly a year had passed, the boy's father told him to fetch his sheep. It was market time and the animals were to be put on the wagon. The boy pleaded with his father to spare the animal. But the father was unmoved.

" 'Son,' the father said, 'this is the way of the world.'

" 'Can we not remake the world?' the boy asked. 'Do not the potters throw new designs on their wheels? Do not the builders search for better foundations, substituting stone for sand?'

" 'You are a farmer's son, not born to power,' the farmer said.

" 'Do I not have the power of one?' the boy asked.

"That day," continued the shepherd, "the man went to market, leaving the sheep in the boy's care. I was that boy. And I vowed that my sheep would never see the cold, sharp edge of the butcher's ax. And so I make my living selling wool."

"Ah," said the Storyteller, "now I know you. A man of his own mind. Thank you for telling your tale."

Elizabeth spoke next. Her voice was as soft as a desert breeze.

❧ *Elizabeth's Tale*

"ONCE THERE WAS a woman of great wealth who lived in a royal house. Her robes were made of silk and her tablecloths were spun with gold thread. She drank from golden goblets and ate from silver platters.

"But she was not happy, and so one day she called her servant girl.

"'Who is greater?' the woman asked her servant. 'The one who sits at the table or the one who serves?'

"The servant remained silent. She did not want to offend the woman. Neither could she lie.

"The wealthy woman pressed for an answer and the girl eventually gave in.

"'My lady,' said the servant girl, 'are those who sit at the table great if they are enslaved to their own selfish needs and wishes? Are those who serve the table less if they are free to love? The giver of love receives. The one who understands is understood. The one who consoles receives consolation. This is the higher law.'

"That day the servant was set free for saying strong things gently and gentle things strongly. The girl went home to visit her dying grandfather, then roamed the countryside until she found work with a merchant. When the merchant disowned his son, the girl took the boy in. I was that girl," Elizabeth said. "Now I am my brother's keeper."

"Ah," said the Storyteller, "now I know you. A

truth teller." The Storyteller thanked Elizabeth for her tale.

"And you, little one?" asked the Storyteller, turning to the boy. "What tale do you tell?"

"Not one with a seeker or a truth teller," the boy said. "This tale is my own. For I am David, son of none. My mother died when I was born. My father beat me, called me stupid and lazy, and one day cast me out. Now I am an orphan without a mother or a home or a birthright."

The boy stopped talking and looked down at his dusty feet. They were red and sore from walking many miles in his weathered old sandals. The leather was scuffed and the laces broken.

"My, my," said the Storyteller, listening to the boy. "This is a sad tale from one so young."

"Do you doubt him?" Elizabeth protested. "The boy speaks from his heart."

"Every narrator makes choices," the Storyteller said. "Some cloak their characters in despair while others choose the garment of hope. Some see the wine jug half empty; others see it half full." He pointed to the carafe on the table in front of them.

"David," the Storyteller said, "where there was sadness, your sister brought joy. Where there was loneliness, the shepherd offered company."

The boy stood straight and still, listening.

"Perhaps you can turn the page and tell a new tale, one in which a new boy walks in new sandals. For the old worn ones have been cast off like the dry, cracked skin of a snake."

The boy was pensive. Elizabeth drew close to his side and took his hand. Then his face lit up and became animated.

"I am David, brother of Elizabeth. Though my mother died when I was born and my father cursed me, I never walk alone. So lucky am I to have my sister and the shepherd, both gentle and kind. And my donkey loves me, too."

"Ah," said the Storyteller. "Not a victim but a survivor. Now we know you. David, the lucky boy."

The Storyteller's Tale

HEIR STORIES TOLD, THE THREE travelers watched the late-afternoon sun begin to disappear. It was time to bed down the sheep and the donkey and retire to a nearby inn. But as they got ready to depart, the shepherd turned to the Storyteller.

"And you, friend. Before we get on our way, would you honor us with a tale?"

Instead of answering right away, the Storyteller stuck out his tongue and wiggled it from side to side, mimicking a serpent poised to strike. Then he told of Kulfi, the Snake Charmer, a man who had eaten from the tree of exceptional knowledge. A man who fasted frequently and slept on a bed of nails. A man whose mere name invoked awe in many who had never laid eyes upon him.

"Do you know Kulfi's tale?" the Storyteller asked.

The Tale of Kulfi, the Snake Charmer

"ONE DAY KULFI announced that he was planning a demonstration. People came from miles around to see the bony little man in the big white turban with the black, bushy mustache. When they arrived, Kulfi was sitting cross-legged on a hilltop, a basket in front of him with a snake inside. He asked everyone to say a prayer to protect him and calm the snake. Then he closed his eyes, sucked in a belly full of breath, and soon the thin, exotic sound of a most sensuous melody was flowing from his flute.

"Time passed but nothing happened. Would the great Kulfi be able to call forth the snake from the basket? People in the crowd began to squirm and grow restless. They had paid dearly for a chance to see Kulfi and they expected a good show.

"And then, just when patience was about to run out—pop! The top of the basket flew up and the head of a snake poked out. It was a yellow and black creature covered with diamond markings, and it zigged and zagged from side to side, seemingly transfixed by the music.

"'Ahhhhhhhhhhhh!' intoned many in the crowd. How did Kulfi do it? What manner of man was he?

"When the viper was completely uncoiled and dancing high in the air, Kulfi leaned forward. The crowd was tense, wondering what this daredevil was going to do next. Then Kulfi stretched out his neck and, drawing dangerously close to the snake, planted a kiss on its head! This was more than anyone had bargained for. The great Kulfi was courting death!

"But one boy was not impressed. Stuck behind a fat lady with copious rolls of flesh, the youngster could not see a thing. Creeping out of the audience, he found a tree and climbed to its highest limb, settling where the sparrows and eagles made their nests.

"From this perch, the boy had a grand view of Kulfi playing his flute. The snake was moving sensuously, the crowd transfixed. It was not clear who was more charmed—the snake dancing to Kulfi's tune or the crowd.

"It was then that the boy saw Dodo, Kulfi's assistant, tiptoeing along the perimeter of the audience. What was this? Were the boy's eyes deceiving him? Could it be that Dodo was helping himself to the pouches and purses of the spectators, slipping their belongings up the sleeve of his tunic?

"'Look!' the boy cried out, 'Dodo the Pickpocket has his hand where it does not belong!'

"'Quiet, boy!' a woman called out. 'You are spoiling the show!'

"Later, when the performance was over, the boy crept up to Kulfi's camp and saw the Snake Charmer and Dodo dividing their stolen loot. Next to Kulfi was the knife he had used to cut out the snake's poisonous glands and the needle and thread he had used to stitch up the reptile's jaw.

"That day," said the Storyteller, "the boy grew leery of crowds that fawn and simper, and of the People of the Lie who charm and seduce. He began to seek the higher ground, with the best view. I know," the Storyteller said, "because I was that boy. Now I look with my own eyes and own my own gifts, as each of us must."

The Storyteller paused and turned to his visitors who were all but ready to leave.

"You are far from home," the Storyteller said. "Where are you going?"

"In search of the new way," the shepherd said.

"Many have gone looking for it," the Storyteller said. "None has returned. Perhaps they were unaware that to find it requires bringing forth what is within you, for what you bring forth will save you."

"Storyteller, you speak in riddles. What is your meaning?" the shepherd asked.

"You will know soon enough," the Storyteller said, "when the last chapter is written and the hero appears."

And with that, the Storyteller closed his book on the day. The travelers thanked him for his generosity and went in search of a place to spend the night.

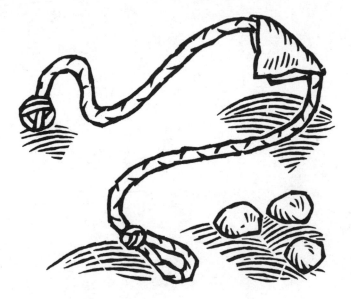

The Unwilling Soldier

HE MYSTICAL GLOW OF DUSK HAD settled on the land. Nobody liked this time of day better than Joshua.

After bedding down his sheep and David's donkey, and settling Elizabeth and David at an inn, Joshua looked out on the horizon. It was a spectacular evening, clear and pleasant. The hot orange sun was beginning to disappear like a trick ball in a magic act, dipping below the distant hills. How often as a child Joshua had lain in a meadow or stood on a mountain, watching the light fade. Now the dusk reminded him to keep his heart as light as a feather.

Like his mother and grandmother before him, Joshua was a simple soul. While others set out in the world to amass great fortunes, build lasting monuments, and leave personal legacies, his hope was to do justice, be merciful, and walk humbly on the earth. He had first felt these stirrings as a young boy, working in the barn, where he doted on the animals like a mother hen with her chicks. It was there that he had come to see life as a great tapestry, with love and caring as its strongest stitches.

Later, as an adolescent, he worked alongside his mother and grandmother in the house. These two women baked bread and carried water, but they were also midwives who birthed the local children. When they packed their donkey cart to go to assist at a delivery, they often took Joshua along to help. On his many excursions he learned how a gentle touch can soothe a woman in labor; how a wet cloth can cool a perspiring brow; how an easy word can relax a nursing mother; and, most of all, how fragile and precious human life is.

When he turned sixteen, the last of these lessons was put to a test.

A royal messenger arrived at the farm on Joshua's birthday carrying a summons of conscription. The King's Defense Force was preparing for war, and Joshua was one of many ordered to leave home and report to the training camp. Those who refused were put in shackles and stoned.

"How shall I fight?" he asked his mother.

She held his hand and cried, but had no answer.

"So this is the sissy," the captain of the guard said when Joshua arrived at camp.

He kicked dust at the young man to see how he would react.

Joshua stood still, saying nothing.

Then the captain tossed a slingshot to the young man and asked him to shoot down a bird. Joshua was unfamiliar with the weapon and fumbled, admitting that he did not wish to kill.

"So I guess we might call you our peaceful warrior," the captain said, laughing. "What good will you be when the enemy invades?"

The young man let the mockery and taunts blow by him like a cool afternoon breeze. But as he watched the captain, he noticed that the military man's horse was frail. Its rib cage was visible and its eyes were glassy. The young man gently stroked the animal, and it lifted its tail and snorted.

"Do you know animals?" the captain said. He was surprised at how aware of the horse's infirmity the young man was.

"This animal needs a special root mixed into its

food right away," the young man said. "We must waste no time."

The captain listened carefully. This was his favorite horse and each day the horse had been losing weight. It would soon be too weak to ride.

He led the boy to the stable and let him examine the rest of the livestock. The boy was extremely knowledgeable about every breed of animal—pigs, goats, chickens, and sheep.

Seeing the boy's tender hand move from cow to pig to dog, the captain decided to petition the king to allow the boy to work in the barn. He was there only a short while but the animals that were sick got well. The sizes of the litters grew larger. And soon the barn was bursting at the seams with new life.

"We must give away some animals to our neighbors," the young man told the captain. The military man was sitting on top of his favorite stallion, newly restored to health, when Joshua made this suggestion. The captain's hard heart had been softened by Joshua's gentle way.

"What will the king say?" the captain wondered aloud. "He would rather give our neighbors a taste of their own medicine."

But after a hearty debate, the king agreed to send a caravan of animals to his enemy. Starving children got milk from the cows. The elderly received eggs from the chickens. Hearts opened that had been closed. And soon there was a truce. The king discovered that he could lead by serving and heal by loving—and achieve surprising and powerful results.

Four years after commencing his military service, Joshua was released by the king and sent on his way with a flock of sheep. He went home to visit his family and then began to walk the countryside, uncertain of his destination. He wandered aimlessly until he saw a man beating his child, a calamity that left Joshua wondering what hope there was for a world where violence flowed as naturally as mother's milk.

The question begged for an answer. He hoped to find it.

But for now, he was tired. The sun had disappeared and had gradually been replaced by a canopy of stars. He went back to the inn, made his way up to the hayloft, and was soon fast asleep.

A Silk Purse from a Sow's Ear

HEY ROSE EARLY, CONSULTED THEIR map, and were walking out to the high road when they heard his voice.

"Mi mi mi mi" came a croaking sound. "Mi mi mi mi." Whoever was singing was so off-key that David covered his ears.

"Mi mi mi mi!" the man continued.

They turned a corner and there he was, standing in front of the apothecary's shop. Bright-eyed, big-bellied, and bald, he was a roly-poly character with beads and shells strung around his waist, and spotted feathers sewn on the shoulders of his garment. Instead of the traditional white tunic favored by men in the hot climate, his tunic was powder blue.

"Oh, my," he said when they came into view. He was not expecting company and was startled.

"I was just exercising my lungs," he explained. "I do it every day to keep myself fit."

He introduced himself as Orion, the Apothecary, and invited them inside his shop for tea. Delighted to be offered refreshment, they entered a disheveled room full of potions, herbs, iron bits, and metal scraps. Signs, mathematical formulas, home remedies, and pithy sayings were painted on the walls. Above a table where he invited them to sit was also a hand-drawn map.

"Where are these cliffs?" the shepherd asked, looking very closely at the rendering. It bore a strong resemblance to Elizabeth's map.

"Above the cave that faces the Great Inland Sea, a few days' journey from here," the Apothecary said. "Sometimes I gather rocks and shells there for my experiments."

"Do you know the cave well?" the shepherd continued.

"Only by reputation," the Apothecary said. "It's a dangerous place, prone to flooding, that attracts seekers of the new way. Many have gone in, hoping to uncover secrets, and none comes out."

The shepherd's eyes widened in astonishment. He was bursting with questions, but David jumped in first.

"What are you making?" the boy asked. He was poking his nose into some copper pots with smoke pouring out of them.

"A silk purse from a sow's ear," the Apothecary said.

"Really?" David asked. Confusion flickered across the boy's face as he waited for an explanation.

"You have been to the slaughterhouse, haven't you?" the Apothecary asked. "It's a nasty place, full of blood and gore. I myself try to avoid it. But once when I was there, I saw a woman pull a sow's ear from the discard pile of skin and guts. Later in the market, she was at her workbench, sewing beads on that strange, coarse thing, turning it into a handsome pouch for a noble lady. A stunning act of transformation. Well, it made me think. If a caterpillar can change into a butterfly and a bud can turn into a flower, what else is possible? Can iron ore be turned into gold?"

"I don't know," said the boy.

"Of course you don't," said the Apothecary. "But you are open-minded. Still fresh to possibilities. The naysayers, with their constant talk of what can't be done, haven't stolen your hopes and dreams yet. Nor mine. I am probing the mysteries and searching for the limits of what is possible."

As the Apothecary spoke, the shepherd thought of the runt he had raised. People had laughed at him when he fetched milk for it. But the runt had grown.

Elizabeth thought of the royal woman who had set her free. People said slaves ought never be forthright to those in power. But Elizabeth had dared to speak out and had earned her freedom.

"What's in here?" David asked. He was poking around a large iron pot that was spewing a thick cloud of white smoke. It curled into the air like fumes from a magic lamp.

"Something I developed for a desperate mother whose child was ill with a mysterious disease," the Apothecary said. "The doctors had given up hope for their young patient. But when the mother begged for my help, I gave her what I would give to any anxious friend—a cup of tea—but I also prayed over it using an ancient incantation. Against all odds, the child got well. Soon people were lining up at my shop, asking for some of my elixir."

The boy had many other questions, but Joshua interrupted.

"The journey ahead is long," he said. "We must be going." The shepherd thanked the Apothecary for his kindness and he and the others got ready to be on their way.

As they were heading out they heard the Apothecary call.

"Woman!" he shouted as he came running out of his shop. He approached Elizabeth and pressed a small pouch into her hand. "This remedy may come in handy. It is very powerful."

Elizabeth thanked the Apothecary for his kindness. And the travelers went on their way.

Seeing Is Believing

BBA AND BABA, JONAH AND IONA, Little and Fiddle, Lev and Zev . . . Zev?

"Where has he gone?" David asked. "I don't see him."

To be a sheep was to live a monotonous life. Grazing, sleeping, drinking, walking, tupping, lambing, wooling. Sheep did little else—except stray from the path occasionally. That seemed to have happened with Zev, the small black sheep with the dewy eyes, and David was fretting over it.

"He probably slipped off to nibble some berries," said the shepherd. "You know what a rascal he is."

David nodded, but he was keen to find the stray and return him to the fold right away. Joshua agreed, and walked back down the hill, descending until he came to a ledge where he saw smoke rising from a campfire. A scrawny man in a loincloth was sitting on the ground, close to the flame, soaking up the heat.

"Hello, old fellow. Have you seen my lost sheep?" Joshua asked.

"I haven't seen anything," said the old man. "I'm blind."

"Ah," said the shepherd. "Sorry to trouble you, friend."

"But I can tell you where your sheep is," said the Blind Man. "Stuck in the bramble bush. Listen."

A rustling noise wafted out of the bushes and after a few seconds, a sheep came trundling out.

"Would you like to clean those scratches?" the Blind Man asked.

"How did you know our Zev is hurt?"

"I see with my ears, feel with my mind, and know with my heart. Have done since I was a boy."

"Strange indeed," the shepherd said. "Yes. It would be good to have water."

"Try the stream beyond the ridge. And do jump in. Very refreshing!"

The shepherd laughed. The Blind Man was proving to be quite an odd fellow. He sat cross-legged on the ground, surrounded by the basic necessities of life—sticks for a fire, berries for breakfast, a few cotton tunics, a water pouch, and a walking stick.

"I am Joshua," the shepherd said, then asked, "Do you live here in the wilderness?"

"Where else?" said the Blind Man. "And yourself?"

"Just passing through on my way to the cave."

"I see," said the Blind Man. "You are searching for the new way. Those who go looking for it don't come back."

Then the Blind Man described the road ahead, plagued by thieves. He urged caution on the path leading to the top of the ridge, where the Great Inland Sea would be visible. And he described what the travelers might expect.

"From there," he said, "the road will wind down. Rest by the shore in the morning—you will need your strength. Then, follow the sun as it moves west, hugging the coast until you see the tall stand of trees. The cave is nearby."

The shepherd told the Blind Man that he had heard about flooding in the cave. The Blind Man listened and then began flapping his hands in the air.

"Pay attention to the birds. They will show you

when the time to enter is right. The birds go inside the cave only when the water is at its lowest, when there is enough air. But be quick! You will have very little time to get what you are after."

"How can I repay you?" Joshua asked.

"Come sit at my fire with your family. Keep company with me."

And so they camped with the Blind Man. They sat by his fire and listened as he told his tale.

❧ *The Blind Man's Tale*

"I WAS BORN BLIND. When my father learned that his son entered the world with two black holes in his head, he told my mother to throw me down the well. 'Do not delay or you will become attached to him,' he said. He was a practical man.

"Knowing she could not obey, my mother quickly

hatched a plan to trick my father. When he went to bed, she wrapped me in a blanket and tied me with a length of grapevine to a large frond. Then she set me in the gentle current of the river and prayed that someone downstream would rescue me. She knew that it was planting season and that the farmers would be out on the banks, tilling the soil early in the morning.

"When my father awoke, my mother told him that she had done as instructed—thrown me into the abandoned well. A fox had come and torn me to pieces, she said.

"Sensing mischief, my father asked for proof. My mother expected that his black heart would want nothing less. She had already gone to the slaughterhouse to fetch the entrails of a pig, which she piled on a plate and set in front of him. Big, rough ninny that he must have been, my father drank his wine and left for work, as if this day were like all others.

"As for me, I floated to a distant place where a family of farmers tilled my soul with friendship and love. Later, when I was grown, my mother sought me out before she died, so sorry was she to have set me adrift."

"Old man," Elizabeth said, "you touch my heart. Will you join us on our journey?"

"A man must walk only his own path," said the Blind Man. "Never another's or his feet will grow tired and sore. And he will feel lost even when he arrives. Your destiny takes you to a different place than mine. But I thank you for your kindness."

The boy was tired. He had curled up among the sheep, finding shelter from the cool night air in their wooly coats, sinking into them and huddling as if they were siblings. He slept closest that night to Zev, the one who had been lost and found.

The Wise Servant

OBODY LIKED THE EARLY-MORNING
sun better than Elizabeth did.

She rose at dawn and went to the
stream and set out fresh clothes.
She picked berries and put the sheep and the donkey
out to graze. By the time the others were awake she
had prepared a table for breakfast. This was her way
of making sure everyone had what they needed.

Like her mother and grandmother before her,
Elizabeth had been born into servitude, and had lived
in the royal house since she was old enough to fill a
pitcher, pick a grape, and carry an earthen jug. She

had often wondered what freedom tasted like, but she was never bitter or unhappy. She kept in mind the tale of the baboons, told to her by her grandmother. The baboons liked to hide in the trees and swoop down whenever the royals were playing their ball game. No matter how hard the royals tried to control them, the baboons picked up the balls and dropped them in random places on the game field. This made the royals adopt new rules and play the ball where the baboons dropped it.

Elizabeth did likewise—she played the ball where it fell, adjusting and making the most of every situation. The respect and influence she earned from her colleagues in the royal house came not from barking orders at the servant girls beneath her, but from finding what worked best for others and helping them to accomplish it.

"Ask Elizabeth," others would say, because they

loved her. She was unceasingly good and relentlessly kind.

The royal lady liked to have Elizabeth at hand. Once, when the court was confronted with an uprising, the royal counselor advocated stern measures to quell the rebellion. When the royal lady dismissed the court she asked Elizabeth to stay behind.

"Why did you hide your gaze when my counselor spoke?" the lady asked.

"Your counselor would fight fire with fire and all would be destroyed by the flames. Better it would be, I think, to be recklessly generous with these neighbors who defy you. For honey tastes sweeter than vinegar."

When the royal counselor heard Elizabeth's recommendation he exploded in rage.

"New rebellions drink from the vine of appeasement," he declared.

The royal lady heard him out. But that day, she

ordered her court to gather spools of the most glorious fabrics and chests of the most exotic spices and the ripest fruit, and deliver them to the warring neighbors. Shortly after, the parties sat down to settle their differences.

As time went by, Elizabeth rose in the royal lady's estimation. Her influence expanded—not because she had a throne or a crown or fine fabrics on her back, but because she told the truth, radiated hope, and loved those around her with her whole heart.

And then the day came when the royal lady set her free. She returned to her grandfather's house, and as the old man lay on his deathbed, he gave her the map and told her of the new way that was waiting to be brought forth. She later went to keep house for David's father.

This day, Elizabeth was preparing breakfast. When David, Joshua, and the Blind Man woke, she served fish from the stream and berries from the bushes. The men and the boy ate heartily. The Blind Man was especially famished and ate like a condemned prisoner consuming his last meal.

"Who knows when I will eat this well again?" the Blind Man said. "And in such pleasant company."

He licked his lips and rubbed his belly. His hunger was gone but now a pain was piercing his heart. His new friends were about to depart for the cave and he was deeply saddened.

"Please, boy, come sit by my fire with me," he said.

"Can you tell another tale, old man?" the boy asked.

The Blind Man felt the shepherd's hand on his shoulder. And so he told a story he had learned as a boy.

"Once there was a wolf so hungry that saliva dripped from his sharp teeth. How that wolf longed to kill a sheep, to have it for supper. How much that wolf would give for a tasty meal.

"But the wolf was frustrated because the shepherd kept watch over his flock, keeping the sheep safe. Why was the shepherd so careful?

"First, because he loved his animals. They huddled with him at night, providing companionship and warmth.

"And, second, he knew that cruel nature had let the sheep be born as the most defenseless creatures in the kingdom. They had no fangs or claws or foot speed or strength to protect themselves against danger, or help them evade it. These sheep could thwart no predator.

"So the shepherd slept with one eye open, making it impossible for the wolf to get close.

"One day the wolf came across a discarded sheep skin.

"'Hmmm,' he thought. 'If I wrap myself in this skin, no one will know that I am a wolf. They will take me for a sheep, and then I will be free to roam where I please.'

"Delighted with himself, the wolf set his plan in motion and was soon in the midst of the herd. When a newborn lamb picked up the scent of its mother on the wolf's skin, and began to trail behind the wolf, it was soon turned into a tasty meal."

The boy shivered.

"What am I to learn from this?" he asked.

"Remember that while there is great good in the world, appearances deceive. Be watchful for the one who comes in sheep's clothing. For that one brings treachery and deceit."

"How will we know the one who comes in sheep's clothing?" the boy asked.

"Stay alert," the Blind Man said. "Listen to your

instincts. Beware the stranger whose smile does not reach his eyes."

The boy thanked the Blind Man for his insights. Good-byes were exchanged and the three travelers went on their way.

Reward and Punishment

HEY WERE ALMOST TO THE CREST when it happened.

"Ooooh! Ouch!" cried the boy.

He began hopping around madly on one foot while clutching the other.

"Take a deep breath now," Joshua said. "And look up to the sky where that bird is circling." When he was sure that the boy was distracted, the shepherd pulled a thorn out of the tender pad of his foot.

"There now, it's all gone," the shepherd said. He rubbed the foot to make it feel better. The boy felt warmth coming from the shepherd's hands.

Joann Davis

Elizabeth moved in to brush David's hair back from his face and wipe away his tears.

"Why?" the boy asked her. "Why am I punished? I said my prayers this morning and did my chores."

Elizabeth did not believe that the boy's suffering was the result of something he had done wrong. Perhaps his father's constant scolding had led David to adopt a bitter view of life. She was eager to substitute a brighter one.

"Look at those storm clouds," she said, pointing to the dark cumulonimbus gathering off to the east. "They may fill our roads with mud today, but their life-giving rain will still make the crops grow. Could it be that all things happen for the best?"

"But this thorn," said the boy. "What good does it do me?"

"Perhaps it will teach you something, make you stronger," she answered.

He nodded and smiled at his sister, who always spoke the truth in love and loved the truth.

They were almost to the top of the ridge. The world was still. The boy was listening. And the cave was just ahead.

The Gift of a Lowly Thorn

HEN THEY REACHED THE CREST, the travelers looked out on the Great Inland Sea. Its sparkling water beckoned them. But it was salty and undrinkable.

"We must find fresh water before we continue," Joshua said. "Our pouches are almost empty."

They needed fresh water so desperately that Joshua suggested he head north while Elizabeth go south. Remembering the Blind Man's cautions, they told David not to wander off—to stay exactly where he was, with the sheep and the donkey—until they returned. They planned to be away for only a short while.

"You have your friends to keep you company," Elizabeth said. "When we return, our water pouches will be full."

"Please, sister," the boy cried. "Hurry."

He was sitting among the sheep, enjoying a faint breeze and whistling to occupy himself, when it seemed to come out of nowhere—a thick, callused hand. It fell on his shoulder and squeezed him.

"So sorry to startle you," said the Stranger, sidling up to the boy. "But I like your tune. I was off in the distance when I heard it and I wondered where you learned such a delicious melody. Perhaps your kind, sweet mother taught you."

"My mother died when I was born," the boy said. "I never saw her face, but they tell me it was lovely and soft. I dream of her at night when the stars are out."

"Poor, sorry boy," said the Stranger. He adopted a tone of sadness and sympathy, but was he sincere?

David looked at the man's face. It was friendly and open. In a way, he bore a curious resemblance to the shepherd. But something was off—the Stranger's smile did not reach up to his eyes. The boy remembered what the Blind Man had told him.

"My sister is near," David said. "Let me summon her."

"No need," said the Stranger. "I can see your lips are cracked from a long walk in the high sun. If you come with me, I will give you all the water you like."

The boy was very thirsty. Here was a generous offer of help. But sometimes looks deceive, the boy remembered. A wolf could be creeping in among the sheep.

The boy looked down at the Stranger's sandals and saw a sharp knife tucked into the laces against the back of his leg. A sick feeling flooded the boy's stomach as the man inched closer.

"Do you like dried fruits and nuts?" the man asked. "Come now and I will share the sweetest delights with you. My camp is just a short ways off."

What the boy wouldn't give for some delicious treats. What did a sweet fig even taste like? It had been so long since one had melted on his tongue that he couldn't remember. This offer from the Stranger posed quite a temptation. He could practically taste the delicious fruit—his mouth was beginning to water. He was weakening, giving in to the idea that this man was sincere and could give him something he really wanted.

Listen to your instincts, the boy remembered the Blind Man saying. *Look at his eyes. What do they tell you?*

"It sounds very delicious," said the boy. "Yes, I will come with you. But I have to get back before my sister and the shepherd return. Or they will not be happy with me."

"Of course," said the Stranger. "I understand completely." But when they turned to walk up the trail, the boy started hopping on one foot, holding on to the other.

"Oooh! Ouch!" he called out. "A thorn. I've stepped on a thorn." Then, like an accomplished thespian in a stage play, he began rolling on the ground, raising a large cloud of dust and spooking the donkey and the sheep. The animals began to scatter in every direction, sending up an even bigger puff of dirt.

The boy continued shrieking, and the Stranger didn't know what to do. He reached for his knife, but no sooner was it drawn than the shepherd arrived.

"Put away your weapon," the shepherd said, raising his staff and holding it out in front of him.

As Joshua planted himself between the Stranger and the boy, his mind flashed back to an image of David in the dirt, covered in welts. It seemed like an eternity since that day in the market when David's father had beaten him. Joshua believed that he had failed the boy that day. It would not happen again. Now, if the assailant lunged, Joshua would take the knife, sacrificing himself.

But as Elizabeth appeared on the path with fresh water, the Stranger took off. He turned and ran, disappearing into the thicket.

"David!" she cried. The boy was down in the dirt and she sat him up and cradled him. He was not especially upset, but tears streamed down Elizabeth's face as she checked him over.

"Do not cry for me, sister," David said, "for today I am a new boy."

"Brother, you mystify me," Elizabeth said. She waited for him to continue.

"Earlier, I stepped on a thorn. Do you recall? I cried, asking, 'Why am I punished?' You told me to remember that each storm cloud carries God's rain. Suffering was a teacher, not a punishment, you said.

"Well, sister, that lesson pricked me like a second thorn. How could a sore foot be my friend? Only today do I realize that it taught me to raise a dust cloud, scatter the animals, and save my life."

David paused and looked out on the landscape, full of thorny thickets. The dust had settled. The Stranger was gone. And the sheep and the donkey were safe and accounted for, each and every one.

When the boy finished speaking, Joshua dried Elizabeth's tears, and they both thanked heaven for David, and for the gift of a lowly thorn.

Raising Doves

N THE THIRD DAY OF THE JOURNEY, they reached the Great Inland Sea. David played on the shore. Elizabeth dipped her feet in the cool water. And Joshua lay down in the sand and rested.

It seemed like an eternity since they had left home, following the shepherd's dream to find the new way. The long, winding road had led them to many remarkable people, each bearing a message.

The Storyteller reminded Joshua of the power of persistence.

The Apothecary said anything is possible.

The Blind Man warned that appearances can deceive.

And the Stranger gave proof that wolves are lurking among the sheep.

It was while contemplating these things that Joshua fell into a deep sleep. He dreamed he was in a faraway place, standing in a meadow.

"You're back," said the wizened Old Man. "But this time you have questions."

"How did you know?" asked the shepherd.

"By that look on your face. You've come to the difficult part."

"Yes," said the shepherd. "I have met the wolf."

"I know," said the Old Man, "and the lamb was threatened. Now you are wondering if a good man can kill a wolf to spare a lamb."

"Many are killed in the name of righteousness," the shepherd said. "That is the way of the world."

"Yes," the Old Man said. "But you seek a new way. You told me so."

The sun was beginning to rise, and a nest of baby doves had begun to sing a morning song, greeting the new day with a gentle melody.

The Old Man cocked his head and listened.

"What if each child was taught from the cradle to sing the song of peace," the Old Man said. "Would the cynics not call it foolish, saying that to be gentle is to be weak? But I tell you that until we are as innocent and pure as doves, our journey will be long and the way dark. Raise doves, not wolves."

Joshua wondered if the Old Man had more to say. But that was it. The dream was done.

Going Inside

OLLOWING THE BLIND MAN'S directions, the travelers had hugged the coastline, heading west toward the trees. Now they stood at the mouth of the cave, a dark and forbidding cleft in the rocks. As they looked into its threatening blackness, beads of sweat formed on Joshua's brow.

"What if I fail?" Joshua asked Elizabeth. "What if I lack the courage and the strength?"

"This is your destiny," Elizabeth told him. "Your dream has called you here."

The shepherd could feel the power of Elizabeth's

love and her confidence in him. That she was with him now made him feel grateful. He fell on his knees to say a prayer of thanks. But almost as soon as his knees hit the ground he heard the boy cry.

"Help, I am being strangled by a giant serpent!"

Joshua went running, but laughed when he saw the boy's predicament. David had somehow gotten coiled up in a powerful vine as he wandered through the lush stand of trees. Joshua studied the vine—and then it occurred to him that so long and strong a growth could be of use. If he secured it at the cave's entrance and wrapped it around himself, he would be better able to find his way back out of the cave.

Elizabeth showed Joshua how strands of the vine rope could be plaited like the hair of the royal ladies to produce a rope of increased strength. Using her slender fingers, she crossed and entwined the strains, moving quickly to produce a long, fortified rope stretching many feet. Joshua believed that if he tied it around his waist and had Elizabeth anchor it to the donkey, standing just outside the cave, that he could navigate the unknown with greater safety.

It was then that they took the map out of the shepherd's side bag and rolled it out in front of them on the ground. Because Elizabeth's grandfather had been an amateur mapmaker, she understood a number of the markings and symbols.

Most significant, she thought, were the markings made in red ink.

"This x signifies a cutout or shelf dug into the rear wall of the cave, probably where jugs and bottles could be placed for safekeeping," she explained, adding that the shelf was the farthest distance from the cave's mouth.

"This z indicates a dangerous pit on the floor where water could flow up and in from an underground stream," she said. She reached out to take Joshua's hand and her face darkened with fear at the thought of him falling into this cavernous hole. Maybe this was the reason no one came out—they had entered the dark cave without knowledge of this gaping hole that could lead to an unknown abyss.

Joshua's mind was racing. First he wanted to know the size of the cave. Was the floor level or tilted? Was there light and air? Other exit points?

He also wondered how high the ceiling was— would he need to crawl? What would he do if a flood came while he was in the rear portion of the cave?

Elizabeth read the legend and estimated that the cave was five hundred paces from front to back. She could not determine if there would be any air in the cave. But Joshua planned to carry a torch and use it to test the air supply as much as to light his way.

She thought the pit was half the distance back

from the entrance to the rear wall. Whether the floor was tilted or level, she could not say.

Joshua thanked her. Now his greatest concern was the possibility of flooding. Then he remembered the Blind Man flapping his hands. *Pay attention to the birds,* he had said. *They will show you when the time to enter is right. But be quick!*

The sky overhead was blue, cloudless, and empty. Joshua tried to be patient, watching the afternoon sun as it moved in its arc across the sky. Then, without warning, a flock of birds flew overhead.

The time had come. The moment was upon him. He prayed for strength to complete the task.

The Time to Act

LIZABETH ANCHORED ONE END OF the grapevine to the donkey and sat on a nearby rock with her hand on the line. Joshua wrapped the other end around his waist and tied it tight. He then lit a torch from the campfire to carry with him.

But before he entered the cave, he needed to speak with Elizabeth. His fondness for her had been growing steadily. The seeds of romantic love were sprouting with each passing day. Now he needed to know if her affection for him was also blossoming.

"Elizabeth," he said. "Many have entered the cave but none has come out. If I survive, I would like to spend my life with you. Will you agree to become my wife?" Joshua asked.

Elizabeth's eyes welled up. "For all eternity," she said. And she kissed him, knowing that his time to act had come.

The two of them called David and told him of their betrothal. He jumped for joy and then watched as the shepherd got ready to face his challenge.

Joshua entered the cave's mouth and inched ahead, keeping one hand on the wall and one hand in front of him, holding the torch. As soon as he got several feet inside the cave, his torch was extinguished by a draft. Now he was confident of the air supply. But he was also walking in darkness, a blind man inching forward in a forbidden place.

The floor began to tilt down as he moved forward.

He walked slowly, counting his paces, feeling for the hole in the cave floor. When he had gone about two hundred paces, he felt a drop-off in the floor with the toe of his sandal, and moved carefully around the edge of the pit. If not for the map, he believed, he would have plunged to his death as many others undoubtedly had.

The cave was cool and damp, but beads of sweat formed on his brow. He pushed forward, testing the vine rope every few paces to make sure it was securely fastened around him. This simple braided rope attached him to the world. Elizabeth's handicraft was his lifeline now, the cord that tied him to all that he knew and loved.

But how long would it be before he reached the back wall? In the timelessness of this place, it seemed like an eternity had passed. Would he ever find what he was after? His hopes and dreams were great. But there seemed to be no reality, just the jutting edges of the cave wall as his fingers dragged along it.

And then—eureka!—there it was. About four feet off the floor was a rectangular cutout in the wall. He estimated that the opening was one foot high and two to three feet across, and must have been meticulously cut by someone with knowledge of the rising water level. Someone with something valuable to store.

But the hole went back farther than his arm could reach. It would take someone smaller—a child—to climb up and in to fully explore it.

In a few minutes he was back outside the cave in the open air. There, standing before him, was David.

A Small Boy's Adventure

HE BOY'S SIZE HAD NEVER BEEN AN
issue. But now Joshua studied
him.

David was short and skinny. He
was also flexible, able to curl up into a small, com-
pact ball. He could certainly get into the hole in the
cave wall to explore what was stowed there. But was
it right to ask him to do it?

When Joshua explained the predicament to Elizabeth, she knew that the boy was the only hope. But
should the boy be put at risk?

That the vine around his waist would break was not an issue. Elizabeth would braid it herself and make sure it was extra strong. That the cave would flood seemed more of a possibility. But Joshua would be right there with David and they would move quickly.

And what about snakes? In the dark, moist cave, a snake could rear its head. But vipers were an ever present danger in their world, not enough to deter them.

"David," she said to the boy. But before she said anything more, David spoke as a man, not a child, declaring his intentions to return to the cave with Joshua.

"What if the light goes out and we are walking in darkness?" Joshua said. "What if you get frightened before we reach the wall or when you are inside the hole?"

But the boy was adamant. "Until now you have

done all for me," he said. "Now it is my turn to do for you."

So they gathered the vines that would be braided into another rope. Then they waited for the birds to fly over. It was the longest wait of Joshua's life.

Out of the Depths *I* Cry to *Thee*

ELLO-ELLO-ELLO-ELLO."

This wasn't scary—it was fun. At least David thought so as he heard his voice echoing through the cave.

The vine had been fastened around his waist and he was walking alongside Joshua as they moved forward into the dark chasm. As had happened before, a sudden draft blew out Joshua's torch and he and the boy were left walking in darkness. Holding the boy's hand made it a slow crawl. But Joshua did not want David to break free and race ahead.

As they inched along, Joshua counted out the paces. This helped him mark progress for himself, avoid the pit, and advise the boy on how much farther they had to go.

But the constant darkness wore on the boy. "How much longer?" he asked.

No sooner were these words out of his mouth than they reached the cutout in the wall. Joshua explained that he was going to hoist the boy up. He would follow a plan that had been carefully rehearsed outside the cave.

"Are you ready?" the shepherd asked, as much to gauge the boy's confidence as his own.

The boy stretched out his hands to scout the area in front of him as Elizabeth had told him to do. Joshua then checked that the boy's waist rope was secure, lifted him up, and tried to keep a hand on him as he crawled into the hole like an earthworm.

How long would it be? Joshua began to sweat profusely. But only a minute had passed when the boy cried out. "I've found something. There's a jug in here."

The shepherd's heart started to race. Could it be that they had it?

He wanted to shout for joy but he waited for David to back his way out of the tight space. Slowly, the boy lowered his feet to the floor and handed off the jug to Joshua. The shepherd wanted to let his fingers linger over this mysterious vessel but he quickly slipped it into his side bag.

"We've got to hurry," said the shepherd. The water was beginning to rush in. There was no time to lose.

A New Law

HEN ELIZABETH SAW WATER TRICK-
ling out of the cave, she panicked.

"Joshua! David!" she called into the cave. But no answer came back.

Inside the cave, water was burbling up from the ground. Within minutes it was up around David's knees. Joshua held the boy's shoulders and tried to guide him, a blind man leading the blind.

"Ouch!" David cried out. "What was that?" A stinging sensation on his right calf radiated out. His leg was beginning to feel numb and then became paralyzed.

It was impossible for Joshua to know what was

happening. He groped around in the darkness until he found a great gelatinous mass clinging to the boy.

"Oooh! Ouch!" cried the boy as Joshua tore the jelly monster off him.

"We are halfway there," Joshua said. "We are almost out. Keep moving."

But the water was rising and the boy was weak. His numb leg was now dragging along, useless. Joshua knew that they were dangerously close to the pit and could easily get swept up by the rushing water. He tried lifting the boy, but as he reached for David, the water came gushing and pulled the boy down.

"Help me! Help me!" the boy cried.

For the first time, Joshua felt the need to find his strength, that inner resource that drove him. He recalled the Storyteller's words:

Bring forth what is within you, for what you bring forth will save you.

"David!" he commanded. "Remember Elizabeth! We must go to her."

Jolted back to his senses, David fought to keep his nose above the water.

"Hold on, David," the shepherd said. Against the rising tide, he clung to the boy who tilted back his head and gasped for air. Now snakes were swarming in a furious pattern. They were slithering around the boy and writhing in a thick pool.

Then, suddenly, the boy felt the tug of his waist rope. Outside the cave, Elizabeth had tapped the donkey and started her walking. The animal was hauling the boy through the water like a little boat on a towline. Joshua finally got hold of the child and was able to secure him, throwing the boy over his shoulder and around his neck like a new lamb. Joshua followed the lifeline fashioned by Elizabeth until he was out into the light and in her arms.

A Fish Tale

AVID TRIED TO BE BRAVE; HE TRIED not to cry. But when Elizabeth examined his leg, he burst into tears. It was numb and covered in a rash. He was exhausted and unable to speak.

Joshua went to get the boy a dry garment while Elizabeth bathed his leg. It was red and swollen, and the numbness was spreading up to the boy's hip. Would he regain feeling in the leg? Would he ever walk again? This illness was unfamiliar. Elizabeth was starting to despair. She wiped the boy's tears.

Suddenly, she remembered the pouch the Apothecary had given her.

"The elixir," she said, looking into David's eyes. "Should we try it?"

The boy nodded and Elizabeth opened the pouch and gave him the special tea to drink. Joshua returned and said a prayer with Elizabeth for the boy's recovery. How long it would take to see improvement was anybody's guess.

But only a few minutes had passed when the boy began to wiggle his toes and bend his knee. "I can stand," he said joyfully, getting up. Elizabeth kissed him and Joshua gave a sigh of relief.

"This is truly remarkable," Elizabeth said triumphantly.

"Anything is possible," the boy said. Then he stroked his donkey and planted a kiss on her snout for helping to rescue him. She snorted and clip-clopped around in a circle.

Now they were all eager to know about the jug. The shepherd had set his side bag down by the cave's mouth, several feet from where they stood. He went to get it and removed the vessel.

It was an earthen jug, brownish red in color, narrow at the neck, and bulbous in the body. It measured about a foot long from top to bottom, and half a foot wide at its thickest section. It was tightly sealed with what looked like a beeswax cork. There was a symbol and some writing stamped into the wax. But Joshua did not understand the words.

"Let me see," Elizabeth said. While at court, she had learned many things, including the stamps and seals of traders, merchants, and esoteric groups who marked their property with distinctive symbols.

She inspected the jug, scrutinizing the seal, and then she called out—

❧ *The Law of Substitution*

"AND THERE'S A SYMBOL of a fish."

"Why a fish?" David asked. Joshua wondered the same.

"At court I learned that the fish was associated with a monastic order that riled the authorities," Elizabeth said. "The image of the fish let people know who was issuing the message."

The shepherd was listening but he was also itching to get the jug open. Elizabeth could see the fire burning in his eyes.

"What next?" she asked.

Joshua picked up a sharp rock and used an edge to slice through the wax. Then, working carefully, he yanked the plug from out of the jug's neck and peered inside, where he could see a parchment scroll.

He asked Elizabeth to use her slender fingers to fish the document out.

It was about five inches across the top and eight inches in length. She laid it carefully on a smooth, dry rock. The edges of the parchment were frayed but it was generally well preserved and easy to read.

Make me a channel of your peace
Where there is hatred, let me sow love
Where there is injury, let me sow pardon
Where there is doubt, let me sow faith
Where there is despair, let me sow hope
Where there is sadness, let me sow joy
Where there is darkness, let me bring light
For it is in giving that we receive
It is in pardoning that we are pardoned
And it is in dying that we are born to eternal life
For this is the Law of Substitution.

The Mysterious Monks

URN FEAR INTO LOVE. REPLACE despair, hate, and heartache with kinder, gentler emotions. Give birth to a glorious new world through simple acts of substitution that replace what is lacking with what is needed.

So here it was—the new way—captured in a prayer that was as poetic as it was profound. Leaving behind the old code of taking an eye for an eye, of fighting fire with fire, or giving perceived enemies a taste of their own medicine, it spoke of channeling peace through acts of goodness, kindness, mercy, and generosity.

As he reflected on the prayer, a great light filled the sky above Joshua's head and a rainbow appeared. Losing himself in its glorious colors, the shepherd saw his entire life pass before him, going all the way back to his boyhood in the barn. How had he not seen it? The Law of Substitution had always been at work in his life, enriching him, making him whole.

Where there was doubt that the runt would live, he placed faith in a better outcome.

Where women suffered in childbirth, his mother and grandmother brought relief.

Where strife and war divided neighbors, the king was merciful, refusing to confuse gentleness and weakness.

Now it was clearer than ever that love was the new way and that continuous acts of compassion could turn the world on its head, dismantling the long-standing code of retribution and spite and ushering in the age of miracles that Elizabeth's grandfather had predicted on his deathbed.

In a flash of insight, Joshua saw compassion not as a reward for the "worthy" or "deserving" but as a salve for the souls of all who were in need. Giving to all. Giving without judgment. Giving without expectation of reward. Unconditionally. *Reckless compassion! Relentless compassion! Offered unceasingly. Until there was no need left.*

In many ways, Joshua thought, Elizabeth's life was a shining example of these principles. Always a model, never a critic, she had shown what kindness meant by taking in David when he had been disowned—pardoning the father who had injured the boy, sowing love where malice had been planted, planting hope where the seeds of despair might be taking root, showering light on the darkened recesses of his vulnerable soul.

And when Joshua was discouraged, Elizabeth and David danced and made music for him, replacing his sorrow with abundant joy. They nurtured his soul with friendship and love, making him whole, much as the family of farmers had done for the Blind Man when they fished him out of the stream as a baby.

It was all clear to Joshua now. The Law of Substitution was the Higher Law that had brought vitality, meaning, and purpose to his every waking moment. It had made him feel cared for and a part of the great tapestry of life.

But Joshua was puzzled. Why had the Law of Substitution been hidden in the dark recesses of a dangerous cave?

From her grandfather, Elizabeth had learned the strange history of the monks whose seal was on the jug. The monks were a contemplative order of freethinkers and mystics, Elizabeth's grandfather had

said. For many years nobody had paid much attention to them. They lived along the shore of the Great
Inland Sea in a sleepy fishing village that had little
contact with the outside world.

But in an instant, everything changed. While out
rowing in a marshy section of the sea of reeds, the
monks discovered papyrus growing abundantly.
Gathering many bundles of it, the monks became
prolific scribes. Their ideas were soon sailing out to
the wider world, carried by the traders and travelers
with whom they made contact.

The authorities who had once ignored the monks
took notice. They watched as the once quiet enclave
began to attract a steady stream of pilgrims who gave
eye-opening accounts of what they had witnessed.
A monk was said to have calmed the rough sea and
walked on water. A monk was said to have cured a
blind man. A monk was said to have fed a large crowd

with a handful of fish and a few loaves of bread.

Issuing a document titled "The Destruction and Overthrow of Falsely So-called Knowledge," the authorities barred the monks from creating new texts or holding public meetings.

"What did the authorities fear?" Joshua asked.

"Any truth but their own," Elizabeth said.

"And the monks," Joshua said, "what did they believe?"

"That hate begat hate," Elizabeth said. "They spoke of forgiveness, love, and healing."

"What happened to them?" Joshua asked.

"Before being driven from their seaside home, they hid their scrolls in caves and set some afloat," Elizabeth said. "And then, mysteriously, the monks vanished, never to be heard from again."

"And your grandfather," Joshua said, "where did he learn of these things?"

"At court," Elizabeth said. "When my grandmother was in servitude, my grandfather worked in the throne room and overheard the high priests discussing the cave."

"Was there talk of the Law of Substitution?" Joshua asked.

"Not of the Law," Elizabeth said, "but of 'the One.' The monks preached that 'the One' would make a difference."

" 'The One'?" asked the shepherd. Confusion flickered across his face. There was so much to absorb. Joshua needed time to think.

But night was beginning to fall. After a long, harrowing day, everyone was tired. Elizabeth put David to bed and said good night. Then Joshua promised the dusk that he would keep his heart as light as a feather. And they all closed their eyes on a most remarkable day.

Tipping the Scales

HE SHEPHERD SLEPT.

He dreamed he was in a far-off place with many open fields, green pastures, and sandlots. The wizened Old Man was there in his usual spot, sitting on his wooden trunk.

"You're back," said the Old Man. "And you are wondering how the change can come about. Or if it is even possible to move from the old way to the new."

"How did you know?" asked the shepherd.

"By that look on your face."

The Old Man took out his balancing scale and

set a heavy stone on one side. This made the opposing, empty scale fly up in the air.

"How can I offset this stone?" the Old Man asked. "It is so heavy."

But the Old Man set to work, scooping up sand from the ground and piling it onto the empty scale. At first nothing happened. But he kept piling on sand until there was a great mound on top of the scale. Slowly, the stone began to lift.

"Do you see?" said the Old Man. "Some results take time. Change can come little by little. But you must hold the vision. And remember the gathering force. For a single grain of sand can tip the scale."

"Yes," said Joshua. "I understand."

Knowing "the One"

———— ❦ ————

 *ESULTS TAKE TIME. HOLD THE VISION. Remember the gathering force.*

The words from the dream were still swirling in Joshua's head when he woke and saw Elizabeth and David at the edge of the shore, scooping up sand, trying to build a tall tower together.

"The sand moves quickly through your fingers," Joshua said as he approached. "Each grain alone seems lightweight and insignificant. Yet one speck can cause the shift. I have dreamed of it."

"Joshua, you mystify me," Elizabeth said. "Tell us what you know."

Joshua described the stone weighing down the balancing scale. "If we keep piling on sand," he explained, "one grain can make the difference."

"Which one?" David asked innocently. Sand was falling like magic dust through his fingers as he spoke.

"Any can be the one," Joshua answered.

"'*The One*'?" David repeated.

And then it was clear. It was not a matter of waiting for a special person to come to make the difference. Everyone had a part to play. Each good act was a tiny miracle. They all added up. All were part of the gathering force that could tip the scale and lift the stone. People everywhere needed to believe and to act.

And if one person acted, one hard heart might be softened, presenting a shining example of what was possible. And by the power of example the change would come!

Message in a Bottle

※

OME. THEY HAD BEEN AWAY FOR SO long that the place had become an idea, a distant memory, a pleasant abstraction. Now, finally, they were going back to the things they knew and loved, and all of them were ecstatic.

"I shall fill a bowl full of delicious figs," David said, "and eat until I can eat no more."

"I will lie in my favorite meadow, beneath the stars," Joshua commented, "and sleep as long as I like."

"I will sit at a table with my dearest friends,"

Elizabeth said, "and talk until we have no more breath."

But first there was an important matter to attend to. In the morning, before setting off, David gathered a bouquet of wildflowers, and Elizabeth and Joshua went before a magistrate in a nearby fishing village to exchange wedding vows. After the ceremony, witnessed by the sheep and the donkey, everyone took a cool swim in the Great Inland Sea and then got ready for the long walk home.

On the way they met them all—the Blind Man, the Apothecary, and the Storyteller. The Blind Man reminded David to keep his eyes open. The Apothecary told Elizabeth to follow her mighty heart. And the Storyteller told Joshua to write a new chapter, as every ending is a beginning.

As they approached home, they also met the Scribe, who was sitting in the market, copying documents. Hearing Joshua's tale of adventure, the Scribe promised to make copies of the Law of Substitution and spread the prayer far and wide. "And when you are older," the Scribe told David, "come back and record *The Book of the Shepherd* with me."

The boy smiled and said he would.

The travelers then carried on to the old homestead where Elizabeth's grandfather once lived. The place was overgrown with weeds and badly in need of repairs. But Joshua saw potential for a small farm. Elizabeth agreed, thinking that she would use the next phase of her life to become a midwife. As for David, he was now keen to learn the ways of a scribe, to read and write.

"Look!" David exclaimed.

They had entered the room where Elizabeth's grandfather had died and it was on the wall—a drawing of a fish. Had it always been there? If so, surely Elizabeth would have noticed, wouldn't she? But there it was, a simple black-ink rendering of the same symbol inscribed on the neck of the earthen jug containing the Law of Substitution. Someone had posted it over Elizabeth's grandfather's bed.

Joshua took the illustration down and discovered a hole dug into the wall behind it. Elizabeth reached inside the hole and drew out a bottle. It was made of blue glass and it glistened in the daylight.

"Shall we open it?" Joshua asked.

"Grandfather would have wanted us to," Elizabeth said. And so she yanked the beeswax plug out of the neck of the bottle and used her long, thin fingers to remove the tightly wrapped parchment scroll tucked inside.

Joshua and David drew close to Elizabeth as she unfurled the scroll. Perhaps it had been written by one of the monks who then set the bottle afloat.

Perhaps Elizabeth's grandfather had fetched the bottle from the sea and hidden it, knowing that the authorities would prefer it destroyed.

It was all speculation. They might never know.

But now they were eager to hear the message. Elizabeth read it aloud:

"Curse not the dark but bring the light.
For God did send help. God sent you."

Joshua helped Elizabeth mount the scroll on the wall of the dwelling where all could see it. And together with David they began to make the old place new.

The Prayer

*M*ake me a channel of your peace

Where there is hatred, let me sow love

Where there is injury, let me sow pardon

Where there is doubt, let me sow faith

Where there is despair, let me sow hope

Where there is sadness, let me sow joy

Where there is darkness, let me bring light

For it is in giving that we receive

It is in pardoning that we are pardoned

And it is in dying that we are born to eternal life

For this is the Law of Substitution.

Afterword

The Law of Substitution is commonly known today as "The Simple Prayer," "The Peace Prayer," and "The St. Francis Prayer," in honor of the medieval monk who was an advocate for the poor, a friend to animals, and a towering model of compassion. The verses of the prayer have also been set to music in the popular hymn "Make Me a Channel of Your Peace," which is beloved by millions.

But the explosive, miraculous power of the prayer is still to be unleashed. That force will be felt when enough of us commit to become the change we wish to see in the world. Don't talk about the change. Make it happen. No one else can make the difference you can make.

Resources

The author is grateful to the following people and sources:

The Gnostic Gospels by Elaine Pagels, which mentions "The Destruction and Overthrow of Falsely So-called Knowledge," and the quote "If you bring forth what is within you, what you bring forth will save you." Both have been adapted for the author's purposes.

Dr. James Gray, who calls upon all to "speak the truth in love and love the truth in each, saying strong things gently and gentle things strongly."

Miriam Lukken, who called my attention to the words "I sent help. I sent you." They are adapted here for the author's purposes.

Gregory K. Jones, author of *Play the Ball Where the Monkey Drops It: Why We Suffer and How We Can Hope.*

James Redfield, author of *The Celestine Prophecy,* for calling my attention to how important it is to reach a "critical mass" and "hold the vision" for change to come about.

Dan Millman, for the phrase "a peaceful warrior."

M. Scott Peck, for the phrase "People of the Lie," which is adapted here for the author's purposes.

The Robert Wood Johnson Foundation, for making me aware of the phrase "reckless generosity."

Ruth Beebe Hill, for making me aware of the phrase "continuous habitual spirituality" from Native American practice.

Joseph Conrad, for his preface to "The Nigger of

the Narcissus" in which he writes of "... that glimpse of truth for which you have forgotten to ask."

The Golden Compass by Philip Pullman, for highlighting the idea that ruling powers often fear "any truth but their own," an idea adapted here for the author's purposes.

Charlotte's Web by E. B. White, for emphasizing the value of the runt, an idea adapted here for the author's purposes.

Acknowledgments

The flaws in this book are mine alone, but many people deserve thanks and praise for the help, support, and love they have offered me along the way.

First to Bob Miller, without whom this book would not exist. When *The Book of the Shepherd* was still a glint in the author's eye, Bob saw it, conceived of what it might be—would be—and shared his vision of possibilities. Thank you, Bob, for your friendship and for finding a place for me at HarperStudio, where you are creating a new and nurturing culture of partnership.

Acknowledgments

To my friends, Cathi and Ron Shapiro, thank you for your faith and goodness. To David Black and his wonderful staff at the David Black Agency, thank you for your guidance and patience. To the extraordinary people who work at HarperStudio—Debbie Stier, Sarah Burningham, Julia Cheiffetz, Katie Salisbury, and intern Martha Batalha—and at HarperCollins—Kim Lewis, Lorie Young, Juliette Shapland, Brenda Segal, Eric Butler, Leah Carlson-Stanisic, Nikki Cutler, Doug Jones, and Mary Schuck—I am happy to be among you. A special thanks to Suzanne Stradley for her sensitive copy-editing.

And to my neighbor Dean Ordway, who has a plaque that reads ". . . don't count sheep, talk to the shepherd," I say thank you for your kindness.

As for the people who sustain me every day in every way, to whom I owe everything, I acknowledge

Acknowledgments

my family. My husband, Kenny, who has always been my partner and my friend, who has always lifted me up and given me love and encouragement where there was doubt and despair, I say thank you. When I don't know much, I know who to ask.

To my mother, Anna, who is a paragon of love. And to Aunt Pearl, who watches over me.

And, finally, to my children, Jenny and Colin, who have always given me that "glimpse of truth" for which I had forgotten to ask. For the two of you, I have no words to express my love and gratitude. Only the steady beating of my heart.

About the Author

Joann Davis, a publishing veteran, is married to the author and historian Kenneth C. Davis. Together they have two grown children, Jenny and Colin, and they divide their time between New York City and Dorset, Vermont.